Dear Matthew—

Wish I could be with the Seder. Hope yours is really special—

Love,

Joel, Karin, Avery, Annie, Jason & Elly

Passover

Haggadah

in Another Dimension

הגדה במימד אחר הגדה של פסח

Including Hebrew and Transliteration

English edition distributed in the US by:
Lambda publishers Inc, ejudaica@msn.com
T: (718)972-5449 F: (718)972-6307

For the Hebrew edition and for other languages
contact: 3d@kippod3d.com (972)-77-4400168

This haggadah was confirmed and approved
by Rabbi Akiva Yitzhaki with a blessing
of Happy Holiday to all Beit Israel

Proceeds from the purchase of this book will be
donated to the children of "Hayim Association" in Israel

ISBN 978-965-91380-1-2

Creator, 3D Producer: Michael Medina
Sculpture and Painting: Emi Sfard
Photography: Eli Neeman
Produced & Published by KIPROD3D

Instructions

Red on left eye **Blue on right eye**

Blessed are You, Lord our God, King of the universe, Who has kept us alive and sustained us and brought us to this happy season.

Kadesh Saying Kiddush

[On Friday night we begin here:

Yom Hashishi: Vayechulu hashamayim veha'aretz vechol tzeva'am. Vayechal Elohim bayom hashevi'i melachto asher asa; vayishbot bayom hashevi'i mikol melachto asher asa. Vayevarech Elohim et yom hashevi'i vayekadesh oto, ki vo shavat mikol melachto asher bara Elohim la'asot.

וַיְהִי עֶרֶב וַיְהִי בֹקֶר יוֹם הַשִּׁשִּׁי. וַיְכֻלּוּ הַשָּׁמַיִם וְהָאָרֶץ וְכָל צְבָאָם. וַיְכַל אֱלקִים בַּיּוֹם הַשְּׁבִיעִי מְלַאכְתּוֹ אֲשֶׁר עָשָׂה וַיִּשְׁבֹּת בַּיּוֹם הַשְּׁבִיעִי מִכָּל מְלַאכְתּוֹ אֲשֶׁר עָשָׂה. וַיְבָרֶךְ אֱלקִים אֶת יוֹם הַשְּׁבִיעִי וַיְקַדֵּשׁ אוֹתוֹ כִּי בוֹ שָׁבַת מִכָּל מְלַאכְתּוֹ אֲשֶׁר בָּרָא אֱלקִים לַעֲשׂוֹת.

On the sixth day **The heaven and the earth, and all their contents were completed. On the seventh day, God finished all the work that He had been doing, and He rested from it. God blessed the seventh day and made it holy, because on that day He stopped from all His work of creation.]**

During the week, we begin here. On the Sabbath, we add the words in brackets:

Baruch ata Adonai Eloheinu melech ha'olam, borei pri hagafen.
Baruch ata Adonai Eloheinu melech ha'olam, asher bachar banu mikol am veromemanu mikol lashon vekideshanu bemitzvotav. Vatiten lanu Adonai Eloheinu be'ahava (Shabbatot limenucha u) moadim lesimcha, chagim uzemanim lesason (et yom haShabbat hazeh) ve'et yom Chag Hamatzot hazeh, zeman cheiruteinu (be'ahava) mikra kodesh, zeicher leyetzi'at Mitzrayim. Ki vanu vacharta ve'otanu kidashta mikol ha'amim. (VeShabbat) umo'adei kodshecha (be'ahava uveratzon) besimcha uvesason hinchaltanu. Baruch ata Adonai, mekadesh (haShabbat ve)Yisrael vehazmanim.

סַבְרִי מָרָנָן וְרַבָּנָן וְרַבּוֹתַי
בָּרוּךְ אַתָּה יי אֱלֹהֵינוּ מֶלֶךְ הָעוֹלָם בּוֹרֵא פְּרִי הַגָּפֶן.
בָּרוּךְ אַתָּה יי אֱלֹהֵינוּ מֶלֶךְ הָעוֹלָם, אֲשֶׁר בָּחַר בָּנוּ מִכָּל עָם וְרוֹמְמָנוּ מִכָּל לָשׁוֹן וְקִדְּשָׁנוּ בְּמִצְוֹתָיו. וַתִּתֶּן לָנוּ יי אֱלֹהֵינוּ בְּאַהֲבָה (בְּשַׁבָּת: שַׁבָּתוֹת לִמְנוּחָה וּ)מוֹעֲדִים לְשִׂמְחָה, חַגִּים וּזְמַנִּים לְשָׂשׂוֹן, אֶת יוֹם (הַשַּׁבָּת הַזֶּה וְאֶת יוֹם) חַג הַמַּצּוֹת הַזֶּה, זְמַן חֵרוּתֵנוּ (בְּאַהֲבָה), מִקְרָא קֹדֶשׁ, זֵכֶר לִיצִיאַת מִצְרָיִם. כִּי בָנוּ בָחַרְתָּ וְאוֹתָנוּ קִדַּשְׁתָּ מִכָּל הָעַמִּים (וְשַׁבָּת וּ) מוֹעֲדֵי קָדְשֶׁךָ (בְּאַהֲבָה וּבְרָצוֹן) בְּשִׂמְחָה וּבְשָׂשׂוֹן הִנְחַלְתָּנוּ. בָּרוּךְ אַתָּה יי, מְקַדֵּשׁ (הַשַּׁבָּת וְ)יִשְׂרָאֵל וְהַזְּמַנִּים.

Blessed are You, **Lord our God, King of the universe, who creates the fruit of the vine.**

Blessed are You, Lord our God, King of the universe, who has chosen us from all the other nations and languages and has made us holy through His commandments. You, God, have lovingly given us, (Sabbaths for rest and) festivals for happiness and joy: (this Sabbath day and) this Festival of Matzot, our season of freedom, (with love,) a holy day to remember how we were taken out of Egypt. For You have chosen us from among all the nations and made us holy. You have given us Your holy (Sabbath and) festivals, with (love and grace,) happiness and joy. Blessed are You, O Lord, who makes holy (the Sabbath,) the people of Israel, and the festivals.

[On Saturday night, we add the following:

Baruch ata Adonai Eloheinu melech ha'olam, borei me'orei ha'eish.
Baruch ata Adonai Eloheinu melech ha'olam, hamavdil bein kodesh lechol, bein or lachoshech, bein Yisrael la'amim, bein yom hashevi'i lesheshet yemei hama'aseh; bein kedushat Shabbat likedushat yom tov hivdalta, ve'et yom hashevi'i lesheshet yemei hama'aseh kidashta. Hivdalta vekidashta et amecha Yisrael bi'kedushatecha. Baruch ata Adonai, hamavdil bein kodesh lekodesh.

בָּרוּךְ אַתָּה יי אֱלֹהֵינוּ מֶלֶךְ הָעוֹלָם, בּוֹרֵא מְאוֹרֵי הָאֵשׁ. בָּרוּךְ אַתָּה יי אֱלֹהֵינוּ מֶלֶךְ הָעוֹלָם הַמַּבְדִּיל בֵּין קֹדֶשׁ לְחֹל, בין אור לְחֹשֶׁךְ, בֵּין יִשְׂרָאֵל לָעַמִּים, בֵּין יוֹם הַשְּׁבִיעִי לְשֵׁשֶׁת יְמֵי הַמַּעֲשֶׂה. בֵּין קְדֻשַּׁת שַׁבָּת לִקְדֻשַּׁת יום טוב הִבְדַּלְתָּ, וְאֶת יוֹם הַשְּׁבִיעִי מִשֵּׁשֶׁת יְמֵי הַמַּעֲשֶׂה קִדַּשְׁתָּ. הִבְדַּלְתָּ וְקִדַּשְׁתָּ אֶת עַמְּךָ יִשְׂרָאֵל בִּקְדֻשָּׁתֶךָ. בָּרוּךְ אַתָּה יי הַמַּבְדִּיל בֵּין קֹדֶשׁ לְקֹדֶשׁ.

Blessed are You, **Lord our God, King of the universe, Who creates the light of the fire.**
Blessed are You, Lord our God, King of the universe, who divides the holy from the worldly, light from darkness, Israel from other nations, and the seventh day from the six days of creation; You have divided between the holiness of the Sabbath and the holiness of the Festival, and You have made the seventh day holier than the six weekdays. You have made Your people Israel holy with Your holiness. Blessed are You, O Lord, Who separates between the holiness of the Sabbath and the holiness of the Festival.]

Baruch ata Adonai Eloheinu melech ha'olam, shehecheyahu, vekiyemanu, vehigi'anu lazeman hazeh.

בָּרוּךְ אַתָּה יי אֱלֹהֵינוּ מֶלֶךְ הָעוֹלָם, שֶׁהֶחֱיָנוּ וְקִיְּמָנוּ וְהִגִּיעָנוּ לַזְּמַן הַזֶּה.

Blessed are You, **Lord our God, King of the universe, Who has kept us alive and sustained us and brought us to this happy season.**

We drink while leaning to the left.

Washing Hands

We wash our hands without saying a blessing.

Karpas Vegetable Dip

We dip a vegetable in salt water and say the following blessing:

Baruch ata Adonai Eloheinu melech ha'olam, borei pri ha'adama.	בָּרוּךְ אַתָּה יי אֱלֹהֵינוּ מֶלֶךְ הָעוֹלָם, בּוֹרֵא פְּרִי הָאֲדָמָה.

Blessed are You, **Lord our God, King of the Universe, who creates the fruit of the ground.**

Yachatz Breaking the Middle Matza

The middle matza is broken in half. The larger piece is the afikoman, which is wrapped up and hidden for the children to find, and which is eaten at the end of the meal.

Maggid Telling the Story of Our Rescue from Egypt

While this next paragraph is said, we lift the seder plate and show the matzot to everyone:

Ha lachma anya di achalu avhatana be'ara deMitzrayim. Kol dichfin yeitei veyeichol. Kol ditzrich yeitei veyifsach. Hashata hacha, leshana haba'a be'ara deYisrael. Hashata avdei, leshana haba'a benei chorin.	הָא לַחְמָא עַנְיָא דִּי אֲכָלוּ אַבְהָתָנָא בְּאַרְעָא דְמִצְרָיִם. כָּל דִּכְפִין יֵיתֵי וְיֵיכֹל, כָּל דִּצְרִיךְ יֵיתֵי וְיִפְסַח. הָשַׁתָּא הָכָא, לְשָׁנָה הַבָּאָה בְּאַרְעָא דְיִשְׂרָאֵל. הָשַׁתָּא עַבְדֵי, לְשָׁנָה הַבָּאָה בְּנֵי חוֹרִין.

This matza reminds us of the poor, meager bread that our forefathers ate in the land of Egypt. Let anyone who is hungry come and eat with us. Let anyone who is needy come and take part in our Pesach meal. This year we are here; next year, may we be in the land of Israel. This year we are subjects; next year, may we be free.

The Four Questions

מַה נִּשְׁתַּנָּה

The matzot are covered, the seder plate is covered or taken off the table for a little while, and the second cup of wine is poured. Usually the youngest child reads the "Mah Nishtanah" (Four Questions):

Ma nishtana halayla hazeh mikol haleilot.
Shebechol haleilot anu ochlin chametz umatza, halayla hazeh kulo matza;
Shebechol haleilot anu ochlin she'ar yerakot, halayla hazeh (kulo) maror;
Shebechol haleilot ein anu matbilin afilu pa'am achat, halayla hazeh shetei pe'amim;
Shebechol haleilot anu ochlin bein yoshvin uvein mesubin, halayla hazeh kulanu mesubin

מַה נִּשְׁתַּנָּה הַלַּיְלָה הַזֶּה מִכָּל הַלֵּילוֹת?
שֶׁבְּכָל הַלֵּילוֹת אָנוּ אוֹכְלִין חָמֵץ וּמַצָּה -
הַלַּיְלָה הַזֶּה כּוּלוֹ מַצָּה!
שֶׁבְּכָל הַלֵּילוֹת אָנוּ אוֹכְלִין שְׁאָר יְרָקוֹת -
הַלַּיְלָה הַזֶּה מָרוֹר!
שֶׁבְּכָל הַלֵּילוֹת אֵין אָנוּ מַטְבִּילִין אֲפִילוּ
פַּעַם אֶחָת -
הַלַּיְלָה הַזֶּה שְׁתֵּי פְעָמִים!
שֶׁבְּכָל הַלֵּילוֹת אָנוּ אוֹכְלִין בֵּין יוֹשְׁבִין וּבֵין
מְסֻבִּין - הַלַּיְלָה הַזֶּה כֻּלָּנוּ מְסֻבִּין!

How is this night different from all other nights?

On all other nights we may eat bread or matza, but tonight we eat only matza.

On all other nights we may eat all kinds of vegetables, but tonight we eat marror (bitter vegetables).

On all other nights we do not dip vegetables even once, but tonight we dip twice.

On all other nights we eat either sitting up or leaning, but tonight, we all lean.

We now begin to tell the story of how the Jewish people went out of Egypt. The seder plate is put back on the table. The matzot should stay uncovered for the rest of "Maggid".

Avadim hayinu lePharaoh beMitzrayim, vayotzi'einu Adonai misham beyad chazaka ubizroa netuya.	עֲבָדִים הָיִינוּ לְפַרְעֹה בְּמִצְרָיִם, וַיּוֹצִיאֵנוּ יי אֱלֹהֵינוּ מִשָּׁם בְּיָד חֲזָקָה וּבִזְרוֹעַ נְטוּיָה.

We were slaves to Pharaoh in Egypt, **but God took us out with a strong hand and with an outstretched arm. Had God not taken our forefathers out of Egypt, then we, our children and grandchildren would still be enslaved to Pharaoh in Egypt. Even if we all were wise and smart and knew the whole Torah, it would still be our duty to tell the story of how the Jewish people came out of Egypt. The more one talks about it, the more praise he or she deserves.**

Five great rabbis Eliezer, Joshua, Elazar the son of Azarya, Akiva, and Tarfon, were once in Benei Berak, talking about how the people of Israel left Egypt. They discussed it the whole night and did not notice that it was already daytime until their students came and told them that it was time for the morning prayers.

Baruch Hamakom, baruch Hu, baruch shenatan Torah le'amo Yisrael, baruch Hu.

בָּרוּךְ הַמָּקוֹם, בָּרוּךְ הוּא. בָּרוּךְ שֶׁנָּתַן תּוֹרָה לְעַמּוֹ יִשְׂרָאֵל, בָּרוּךְ הוּא.

Blessed be God; **blessed be He who has given the Torah to His people Israel.**

The Four Children

The Torah refers to four types of children: wise, wicked, simple, and one who does not know how to ask a question.

What does the wise child say? **"What is the meaning of these rules that God gave us?" We teach him or her all the laws of Passover, including the eating of the Afikoman.**

What does the wicked child say? **"Why are you doing all this hard work?" He says "you" and does not include himself in the community, which is very important in Judaism. So we tell him or her bluntly: "We do the seder because of what God did for us when we came out of Egypt; had you been there, you would not have been freed from slavery."**

What does the simple child say? **"What is this?" We tell him or her that this is to remember that God took us out of Egypt, where we were slaves, with a strong hand.**

As for the fourth child, **we do not wait for him or her to ask. Instead, we explain that we have a seder to remember what God did for us when He took us out of Egypt.**

At first, **our forefathers bowed down to false gods, but now God has brought us close to Him, as it says: "So said the Lord, God of Israel: A long time ago, your forefathers - Terach, father of Abraham and father of Nachor - lived on the other side of the Euphrates River and bowed down to other gods. Then I took your father Abraham from there and led him into the whole land of Canaan and gave him many children. I gave him Isaac, and to Isaac I gave Jacob and Esau. I gave Esau Mount Seir, while Jacob and his children went down to Egypt."**

Blessed is God, **Who keeps His promise to Israel. For He planned the time that He would take the people of Israel out of Egypt in order to keep His promise to Abraham, as it says: "Know that your children will be strangers**

in someone else's land, where they will be slaves and be tortured for four hundred years; but in the end they will go free with great wealth."

The wicked

The wise

The one who doesn't know how to ask

The simpleton

The matzot are covered and the cup of wine is raised.

Vehi she'amda la'avoteinu velanu.	וְהִיא שֶׁעָמְדָה לַאֲבוֹתֵינוּ וְלָנוּ!
Shelo echad bilvad amad aleinu lechaloteinu	שֶׁלֹּא אֶחָד בִּלְבָד עָמַד עָלֵינוּ לְכַלּוֹתֵנוּ,
ela shebechol dor vador omdim aleinu lechaloteinu,	אֶלָּא שֶׁבְּכָל דּוֹר וָדוֹר עוֹמְדִים עָלֵינוּ לְכַלּוֹתֵנוּ,
veHakadosh Baruch Hu matzileinu miyadam.	וְהַקָּדוֹשׁ בָּרוּךְ הוּא מַצִּילֵנוּ מִיָּדָם.

This promise that God made to Abraham has stood the test of time –

not only for our forefathers in Egypt, but in every age.

There are those who try to destroy us in every generation,

but God always saves us.

The cup of wine is put down and the matzot are uncovered.

Go and learn:

The Haggadah tells the story of how we went out of Egypt in four short verses from the Torah,
and invites us to discuss their meanings:

"My father was a wandering Aramean. He went down to Egypt and lived there, few in number. But there he became a great, mighty, and numerous nation."

My father was a wandering Aramean

in Hebrew this can also be read as "an Aramean tried to destroy my father" - meaning that Laban of Aram tried to destroy our father Jacob and his whole family,

He went down to Egypt and lived there

Jacob and his family went to live in Egypt during the famine in his homeland of Canaan (Israel). He did not want to settle there, only to live there for a little while until the famine would be over.

וַיְעַנּוּנוּ, וַיִּתְּנוּ

"The Egyptians treated us roughly, tormented us, and gave us hard work."

few in number

they were a family of only seventy people when they arrived in Egypt and they were called the Children of Israel.

But there he became a ... nation

they kept their separate identity and culture, language, and customs even in Egypt.

Great, mighty, and numerous

they increased greatly in numbers and power.

"The Egyptians treated us roughly, tormented us, and gave us hard work."

The Egyptians treated us roughly

they were afraid that the Israelites were becoming too powerful and would join the enemies of Egypt to try to escape.

Tormented us and gave us hard work

they made us their slaves and made us build Pharaoh's storage cities. they put guards over us who tormented us.

"And we cried to the Lord, God of our forefathers, and God heard our voice, and saw our torment, hard work, and oppression."

ונצעק

And we cried to the Lord, God of our forefathers, and God heard our voice

when God heard our cries, He remembered the promise he had made to Abraham, Isaac, and Jacob to free the people of Israel and bring them back to their land.

and saw our torment, hard work, and oppression

God saw that the Egyptians were making the lives of the Israelites miserable. Not only that, but Pharaoh ordered that every son born to the Israelites should be killed.

"And God brought us out of Egypt with a mighty hand and outstretched arm, with great terror, and with signs and miracles."

God brought us out of Egypt

not through an angel, nor through an agent, nor through a messenger. But God Himself took us out. As it says:

"I will pass through the land of Egypt on that night:
I and not an agent;
I will strike all the firstborn in the land of Egypt:
I and not an angel;
And on all the gods of Egypt I will execute judgments:
I and not a messenger;
I am the Lord: I and no other."

with a mighty hand and outstretched arm, with great terror, and with signs

God made all kinds of great miracles and terrible plagues that showed the Egyptians and the people of Israel that He is the true God Who rules the world.

Three drops of wine are spilled from the cup (with one's finger) while saying "blood, fire, and pillars of smoke".

and with miracles:

as it says: "I will show miracles in the sky and on the earth:

blood, fire, and pillars of smoke."

Once again, we spill a drop of wine from the cup while saying each of the ten plagues:

These are the ten plagues that God brought upon the Egyptians in Egypt:

Blood	דָּם
Frogs	צְפַרְדֵּעַ
Lice	כִּנִּים
Wild Animals	עָרוֹב
Death of the animals	דֶּבֶר
Boils / Blisters	שְׁחִין
Hail	בָּרָד
Locusts	אַרְבֶּה
Darkness	חֹשֶׁךְ
Death of the Firstborn	מַכַּת בְּכוֹרוֹת

Rabbi Judah remembered the ten plagues by using the first letter of each plague (in Hebrew) to spell:

Detzach, Adash, Be'achab

The plagues convinced Pharaoh to let the people of Israel go free.
But when they left he changed his mind, and sent his soldiers after them.
The song "Dayyenu" tells the rest of the story

Dam, Tzefarde'a, Kinim, Arov, Dever, Shechin, Barad, Arbeh, Choshech, Makat bechorot

דצ״ך עד״ש

באח״ב

Dayyenu (it would have been enough)

How many great things has God done for us!

Had He only brought us out of Egypt, Dayyenu

Had He only punished the Egyptians, Dayyenu

Had He only punished their gods, Dayyenu

Had He only killed their firstborns, Dayyenu

Had He only given us their riches, Dayyenu

Had He only split the sea for us, Dayyenu

Had He only led us across it on dry land, Dayyenu

Had He only drowned our enemies in it, Dayyenu

Had He only taken care of us in the desert for forty years, Dayyenu

Had He only fed us manna, Dayyenu

Had He only given us the Sabbath, Dayyenu

Had He only brought us to Mount Sinai, Dayyenu

Had He only given us the Torah, Dayyenu

Had He only brought us into the land of Israel,
and not built the Holy Temple for us, Dayyenu

God has done all these things for us and for this we must thank Him!

Ilu hotzi'anu miMitzrayim,
Ilu asa bahem shefatim,
Ilu asa be'eloheihem,
Ilu harag et bechoreihem,
Ilu natan lanu et mamonam,
Ilu kara lanu at hayam,
Ilu he'eviranu betocho bechorava,
Ilu shika tzareinu betocho,
Ilu sipeik tzarkeinu bamidbar arba'im shana,
Ilu he'echilanu et haman,
Ilu natan lanu et haShabbat,
Ilu kervanu lifnei Har Sinai,
Ilu natan lanu et haTorah,
Ilu hechnisanu leEretz Yisrael, velo bana lanu et Beit HaBechira

אִלּוּ הוֹצִיאָנוּ מִמִּצְרַיִם וְלֹא עָשָׂה בָּהֶם שְׁפָטִים, דַּיֵּנוּ.
אִלּוּ עָשָׂה בָּהֶם שְׁפָטִים, וְלֹא עָשָׂה בֵאלֹהֵיהֶם, דַּיֵּנוּ.
אִלּוּ עָשָׂה בֵאלֹהֵיהֶם, וְלֹא הָרַג אֶת בְּכוֹרֵיהֶם, דַּיֵּנוּ.
אִלּוּ הָרַג אֶת בְּכוֹרֵיהֶם וְלֹא נָתַן לָנוּ אֶת מָמוֹנָם, דַּיֵּנוּ.
אִלּוּ נָתַן לָנוּ אֶת מָמוֹנָם וְלֹא קָרַע לָנוּ אֶת הַיָּם, דַּיֵּנוּ.
אִלּוּ קָרַע לָנוּ אֶת הַיָּם וְלֹא הֶעֱבִירָנוּ בְתוֹכוֹ בֶּחָרָבָה, דַּיֵּנוּ.
אִלּוּ הֶעֱבִירָנוּ בְתוֹכוֹ בֶּחָרָבָה וְלֹא שִׁקַּע צָרֵנוּ בְּתוֹכוֹ, דַּיֵּנוּ.
אִלּוּ שִׁקַּע צָרֵנוּ בְּתוֹכוֹ וְלֹא סִפֵּק צָרְכֵּנוּ בַּמִּדְבָּר אַרְבָּעִים שָׁנָה, דַּיֵּנוּ.
אִלּוּ סִפֵּק צָרְכֵּנוּ בַּמִּדְבָּר אַרְבָּעִים שָׁנָה וּלֹא הֶאֱכִילָנוּ אֶת הַמָּן, דַּיֵּנוּ.
אִלּוּ הֶאֱכִילָנוּ אֶת הַמָּן וְלֹא נָתַן לָנוּ אֶת הַשַּׁבָּת, דַּיֵּנוּ.
אִלּוּ נָתַן לָנוּ אֶת הַשַּׁבָּת, וְלֹא קֵרְבָנוּ לִפְנֵי הַר סִינַי, דַּיֵּנוּ.
אִלּוּ קֵרְבָנוּ לִפְנֵי הַר סִינַי, וְלֹא נָתַן לָנוּ אֶת הַתּוֹרָה, דַּיֵּנוּ.
אִלּוּ נָתַן לָנוּ אֶת הַתּוֹרָה וְלֹא הִכְנִיסָנוּ לְאֶרֶץ יִשְׂרָאֵל, דַּיֵּנוּ.
אִלּוּ הִכְנִיסָנוּ לְאֶרֶץ יִשְׂרָאֵל וְלֹא בָנָה לָנוּ אֶת בֵּית הַבְּחִירָה, דַּיֵּנוּ.

Rabbi Gamliel used to say: **whoever does not mention these three things on Passover has not fulfilled his duty:**

פֶּסַח, מַצָּה וּמָרוֹר

The Passover offering, matza, and marror

Why did our forefathers eat the Passover offering when the Temple still stood?

Because God passed over the houses of our forefathers in Egypt when He punished the Egyptians, saving our homes.

The matza is shown while we say:

Why do we eat this matza?

Because the dough which our forefathers prepared had no time to rise before God appeared to them and set them free; they were chased out of Egypt and could not delay.

The marror is shown while we say:

Why do we eat this marror (bitter vegetable)?

Because the Egyptians made the lives of our forefathers in Egypt bitter with the hard work of cement, bricks, and every type of field work. All the work they made them do was harsh.

In every generation, we must see ourselves as though we went out of Egypt,

as it says: "You shall tell your child on that day: 'It is because of all that God did for me when I went out of Egypt.'" It is not only our forefathers whom God redeemed, but us too, as it says: "And he took us out of there in order to bring us and to give us the land that he swore to our forefathers."

We lift our cups and cover the matzot while saying:

Therefore, we must give praise and thanks to God because He did all these miracles for our forefathers and for us: He took us from slavery to freedom, from sadness to happiness, from mourning to celebration, and from darkness to great light. So let us sing a new song to Him: Halleluyah! (Praise God!)

Halleluyah!

הַלְלוּ עַבְדֵי יי, הַלְלוּ אֶת שֵׁם יי.
יְהִי שֵׁם יי מְבֹרָךְ מֵעַתָּה וְעַד עוֹלָם.

Hallelu avdei Adonai; hallelu et Shem Adonai.
Yehi Shem Adonai mevorach me'ata ve'ad olam

Give praise, O servants of God; praise God's Name. Let God's Name be blessed now and forever.

בְּצֵאת יִשְׂרָאֵל מִמִּצְרָיִם,

בֵּית יַעֲקֹב מֵעַם לֹעֵז, הָיְתָה
יְהוּדָה לְקָדְשׁוֹ, יִשְׂרָאֵל
מַמְשְׁלוֹתָיו. הַיָּם רָאָה וַיָּנֹס,
הַיַּרְדֵּן יִסֹּב לְאָחוֹר. הֶהָרִים רָקְדוּ
כְאֵילִים, גְּבָעוֹת - כִּבְנֵי צֹאן.
מַה לְּךָ הַיָּם כִּי תָנוּס, הַיַּרְדֵּן -
תִּסֹּב לְאָחוֹר, הֶהָרִים - תִּרְקְדוּ
כְאֵילִים, גְּבָעוֹת - כִּבְנֵי צֹאן.
מִלִּפְנֵי אָדוֹן חוּלִי אָרֶץ, מִלִּפְנֵי
אֱלוֹהַּ יַעֲקֹב. הַהֹפְכִי הַצּוּר אֲגַם
מָיִם, חַלָּמִישׁ - לְמַעְיְנוֹ מָיִם.

Betzeit Yisrael miMitzrayim beit Ya'akov mei'am lo'ez, hayeta Yehuda lekodsho Yisrael mamshelotav. Hayam ra'a vayanos, haYarden yisov le'achor. Heharim rakdu che'eilim, geva'ot kivnei tzon. Ma lecha hayam ki tanus, haYarden tisov le'achor? Heharim tirkedu che'eilim, geva'ot kivnei tzon? Milifnei adon chuli aretz, milifnei Eloha Ya'akov, hahofechi hatzur agam mayim, chalamish lema'ayno mayim.

When Israel went out of Egypt,

the family of Jacob from a foreign nation, Judah became His holy one; the children of Israel his subjects. The sea saw them and ran away, the Jordan River flowed backwards; the mountains danced like rams; the hills like sheep. What is the matter with you,

O sea, that you run away? O Jordan, that you run backwards?

O mountains, that you dance like rams; O hills, like sheep? We tremble at the presence of the Lord, God of Jacob, Who turned rock into a pool of water and stone into a spring of water.

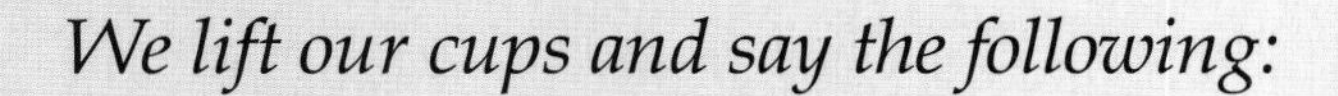
We lift our cups and say the following:

Baruch ata Adonai Eloheinu melech ha'olam, asher ga'alanu vega'al et avoteinu miMitzrayim, vehigi'anu lalayla hazeh le'echol bo matza umaror
Baruch ata Adonai Eloheinu melech ha'olam, borei pri hagafen.

בָּרוּךְ אתה יי אֱלהֵינוּ מֶלֶךְ העוֹלָם,
אֲשֶׁר גְּאָלָנוּ וְגָאַל אֶת אֲבוֹתֵינוּ
מִמִּצְרַיִם, וְהִגִּיעָנוּ לַלַּיְלָה הַזֶּה לֶאֱכָל
בּוֹ מַצָּה וּמָרוֹר.
בָּרוּךְ אַתָּה יי אֱלהֵינוּ מֶלֶךְ הָעוֹלָם
בּוֹרֵא פְּרִי הַגָּפֶן.

Blessed are You, **Lord our God, King of the universe, Who has redeemed us and our forefathers from Egypt and who helped us to reach this night that we may eat matza and marror. So may the Lord our God, God of our forefathers, help us to reach other festivals and other holidays peacefully, celebrate the rebuilding of Jerusalem, and be happy in Your service. May we eat of the sacrifices and Passover offerings in Your Temple. We shall praise You with a new song for our freedom and for the rescue of our lives. Blessed are You, God, who has redeemed Israel.**

Blessed are You, **Lord our God, King of the universe, Who creates the fruit of the vine.**

We drink while leaning to the left.

Rachtza Hand Washing

We wash our hands and say the following blessing.

Baruch ata Adonai Eloheinu melech ha'olam, asher kideshanu bemitzvotav vetzivanu, al netilat yadayim.

בָּרוּךְ אַתָּה יי אֱלהֵינוּ מֶלֶךְ הָעוֹלָם,
אֲשֶׁר קִדְּשָׁנוּ בְּמִצְוֹתָיו וְצִוָּנוּ עַל
נְטִילַת יָדַיִם.

Blessed are You, **Lord our God, King of the Universe, Who has made us holy with His commandments and commanded us to wash hands.**

Motzi Matza Eating the Matza מוֹצִיא, מַצָּה

All three matzot are held together while saying the first blessing. After that, the bottom matza is put down and the second blessing is said while holding the other two matzot, which are then given out. Everyone should eat a piece while leaning to the left.

Baruch ata Adonai Eloheinu melech ha'olam, hamotzi lechem min ha'aretz.
Baruch ata Adonai Eloheinu melech ha'olam, asher kideshanu bemitzvotav vetzivanu al achilat matza.

בָּרוּךְ אַתָּה יי אֱלֹהֵינוּ מֶלֶךְ הָעוֹלָם הַמּוֹצִיא לֶחֶם מִן הָאָרֶץ.
בָּרוּךְ אַתָּה יי אֱלֹהֵינוּ מֶלֶךְ הָעוֹלָם, אֲשֶׁר קִדְּשָׁנוּ בְּמִצְוֹתָיו וְצִוָּנוּ עַל אֲכִילַת מַצָּה.

Blessed are You, **Lord our God, King of the Universe who brings forth bread from the ground.**
Blessed are You, Lord our God, King of the Universe, who has made us holy with His commandments and commanded us to eat matza.

Marror Eating the Bitter Vegetable

We take some marror, dip it into the charoset, say the blessing, and then eat the two together. Since the marror reminds us of slavery, we do not lean while eating it.

Baruch ata Adonai Eloheinu melech ha'olam, asher kideshanu bemitzvotav vetzivanu al achilat maror.	בָּרוּךְ אַתָּה יי אֱלֹהֵינוּ מֶלֶךְ הָעוֹלָם, אֲשֶׁר קִדְּשָׁנוּ בְּמִצְוֹתָיו וְצִוָּנוּ עַל אֲכִילַת מָרוֹר.

Blessed are You, **Lord our God, King of the Universe, who has made us holy with His commandments and commanded us to eat marror.**

Korech The Sandwich

We take a piece of matza and use it to make a sandwich with the marror. It is eaten while leaning. The following is said before eating:

This is to remember what was done in the Temple, according to Hillel: While the Temple still stood, Hillel would wrap the Passover offering and marror into the matza and eat them together, to fulfill what is said: "They shall eat it with matza and marror."

Shulchan Orech

The Festive Meal

We now eat the holiday meal. Many families have special foods - hard-boiled eggs, for example - that they serve at the seder. Make sure to save some room for the afikoman!

Tzafun Finding the Hidden Matza

At the end of the meal, we find the afikoman and everyone eats a piece.

Barech The Grace after Meals

The third cup of wine is poured.

שִׁיר הַמַּעֲלוֹת בְּשׁוּב יי אֶת שִׁיבַת צִיּוֹן הָיִינוּ כְּחֹלְמִים. אָז יִמָּלֵא שְׂחוֹק פִּינוּ וּלְשׁוֹנֵנוּ רִנָּה: אָז יֹאמְרוּ בַגּוֹיִם הִגְדִּיל יי לַעֲשׂוֹת עִם אֵלֶּה. הִגְדִּיל יי לַעֲשׂוֹת עִמָּנוּ הָיִינוּ שְׂמֵחִים. שׁוּבָה יי אֶת שְׁבִיתֵנוּ כַּאֲפִיקִים בַּנֶּגֶב. הַזֹּרְעִים בְּדִמְעָה בְּרִנָּה יִקְצֹרוּ. הָלוֹךְ יֵלֵךְ, וּבָכֹה נֹשֵׂא מֶשֶׁךְ הַזָּרַע: בֹּא יָבֹא בְרִנָּה נֹשֵׂא אֲלֻמֹּתָיו.

בִּרְכַּת הַמָּזוֹן רַבּוֹתַי נְבָרֵךְ. יְהִי שֵׁם יי מְבוֹרָךְ מֵעַתָּה וְעַד עוֹלָם. בִּרְשׁוּת מָרָנָן וְרַבּוֹתַי, נְבָרֵךְ שֶׁאָכַלְנוּ מִשֶּׁלוֹ.
בָּרוּךְ שֶׁאָכַלְנוּ מִשֶּׁלוֹ וּבְטוּבוֹ חָיִינוּ. בָּרוּךְ שֶׁאָכַלְנוּ מִשֶּׁלוֹ וּבְטוּבוֹ חָיִינוּ.
בָּרוּךְ הוּא וּבָרוּךְ שְׁמוֹ.

בָּרוּךְ אַתָּה יי אֱלֹהֵינוּ מֶלֶךְ הָעוֹלָם הַזָּן אֶת הָעוֹלָם כֻּלּוֹ בְּטוּבוֹ בְּחֵן בְּחֶסֶד וּבְרַחֲמִים הוּא נוֹתֵן לֶחֶם לְכָל בָּשָׂר כִּי לְעוֹלָם חַסְדּוֹ. וּבְטוּבוֹ הַגָּדוֹל תָּמִיד לֹא חָסַר לָנוּ, וְאַל יֶחְסַר לָנוּ מָזוֹן לְעוֹלָם וָעֶד. בַּעֲבוּר שְׁמוֹ הַגָּדוֹל, כִּי הוּא אֵל זָן וּמְפַרְנֵס לַכֹּל וּמֵטִיב לַכֹּל, וּמֵכִין מָזוֹן לְכָל בְּרִיּוֹתָיו אֲשֶׁר בָּרָא. בָּרוּךְ אַתָּה יי הַזָּן אֶת הַכֹּל.

Baruch ata Adonai Eloheinu melech ha'olam, hazan et ha'olam kulo betuvo bechein bechesed uverachamim. Hu notein lechem lechol basar ki le'olam chasdo. Uvetuvo hagadol tamid lo chaser lanu, ve'al yechsar lanu mazon le'olam va'ed. Ba'avur shemo hagadol. Ki Hu El zan umefarnes lakol umeitiv lakol umeichin mazon lechol beriyotav asher bara. Baruch ata Adonai, hazan et hakol.

Blessed are You, **Lord our God, King of the Universe, who feeds the whole world with His goodness, with love, with kindness, and with compassion. He gives food to all creatures, for His kindness is forever. Since He is so good, we never lacked and will never lack food. We ask for this so that we can praise His great Name, because He is the God Who feeds everyone and does good for everyone. He prepares food for all of His creatures. Blessed are You, God, who feeds all.**

נוֹדֶה לְךָ יי אֱלֹהֵינוּ עַל שֶׁהִנְחַלְתָּ לַאֲבוֹתֵינוּ אֶרֶץ חֶמְדָּה טוֹבָה וּרְחָבָה, וְעַל שֶׁהוֹצֵאתָנוּ יי אֱלֹהֵינוּ מֵאֶרֶץ מִצְרַיִם, וּפְדִיתָנוּ מִבֵּית עֲבָדִים, וְעַל בְּרִיתְךָ שֶׁחָתַמְתָּ בִּבְשָׂרֵנוּ, וְעַל תּוֹרָתְךָ שֶׁלִּמַּדְתָּנוּ, וְעַל חֻקֶּיךָ שֶׁהוֹדַעְתָּנוּ, וְעַל חַיִּים חֵן וָחֶסֶד שֶׁחוֹנַנְתָּנוּ, וְעַל אֲכִילַת מָזוֹן שָׁאַתָּה זָן וּמְפַרְנֵס אוֹתָנוּ תָּמִיד, בְּכָל יוֹם וּבְכָל עֵת וּבְכָל שָׁעָה: וְעַל הַכֹּל יי אֱלֹהֵינוּ אֲנַחְנוּ מוֹדִים לָךְ וּמְבָרְכִים אוֹתָךְ, יִתְבָּרַךְ שִׁמְךָ בְּפִי כָּל חַי תָּמִיד לְעוֹלָם וָעֶד: כַּכָּתוּב, וְאָכַלְתָּ וְשָׂבָעְתָּ וּבֵרַכְתָּ אֶת יי אֱלֹהֶיךָ עַל הָאָרֶץ הַטּוֹבָה אֲשֶׁר נָתַן לָךְ. בָּרוּךְ אַתָּה יי עַל הָאָרֶץ וְעַל הַמָּזוֹן:

רַחֵם נָא יי אֱלֹהֵינוּ עַל יִשְׂרָאֵל עַמֶּךָ וְעַל יְרוּשָׁלַיִם עִירֶךָ וְעַל צִיּוֹן מִשְׁכַּן כְּבוֹדֶךָ וְעַל מַלְכוּת בֵּית דָּוִד מְשִׁיחֶךָ וְעַל הַבַּיִת הַגָּדוֹל וְהַקָּדוֹשׁ שֶׁנִּקְרָא שִׁמְךָ עָלָיו: אֱלֹהֵינוּ אָבִינוּ, רְעֵנוּ זוּנֵנוּ פַּרְנְסֵנוּ וְכַלְכְּלֵנוּ וְהַרְוִיחֵנוּ, וְהַרְוַח לָנוּ יי אֱלֹהֵינוּ מְהֵרָה מִכָּל צָרוֹתֵינוּ. וְנָא אַל תַּצְרִיכֵנוּ יי אֱלֹהֵינוּ, לֹא לִידֵי מַתְּנַת בָּשָׂר וָדָם וְלֹא לִידֵי הַלְוָאָתָם, כִּי אִם לְיָדְךָ הַמְּלֵאָה הַפְּתוּחָה הַקְּדוֹשָׁה וְהָרְחָבָה, שֶׁלֹּא נֵבוֹשׁ וְלֹא נִכָּלֵם לְעוֹלָם וָעֶד.

וְאִם חָל בְּשַׁבָּת מוֹסִיפִים:

רְצֵה וְהַחֲלִיצֵנוּ יי אֱלֹהֵינוּ בְּמִצְוֹתֶיךָ וּבְמִצְוַת יוֹם הַשְּׁבִיעִי הַשַּׁבָּת הַגָּדוֹל וְהַקָּדוֹשׁ הַזֶּה. כִּי יוֹם זֶה גָּדוֹל וְקָדוֹשׁ הוּא לְפָנֶיךָ לִשְׁבָּת בּוֹ וְלָנוּחַ בּוֹ בְּאַהֲבָה כְּמִצְוַת רְצוֹנֶךָ. וּבִרְצוֹנְךָ הָנִיחַ לָנוּ יי אֱלֹהֵינוּ שֶׁלֹּא תְהֵא צָרָה וְיָגוֹן וַאֲנָחָה בְּיוֹם מְנוּחָתֵנוּ. וְהַרְאֵנוּ יי אֱלֹהֵינוּ בְּנֶחָמַת צִיּוֹן עִירֶךָ וּבְבִנְיַן יְרוּשָׁלַיִם עִיר קָדְשֶׁךָ כִּי אַתָּה הוּא בַּעַל הַיְשׁוּעוֹת וּבַעַל הַנֶּחָמוֹת.

אֱלֹהֵינוּ וֵאלֹהֵי אֲבוֹתֵינוּ, יַעֲלֶה וְיָבֹא וְיַגִּיעַ וְיֵרָאֶה וְיֵרָצֶה וְיִשָּׁמַע וְיִפָּקֵד וְיִזָּכֵר זִכְרוֹנֵנוּ וּפִקְדוֹנֵנוּ, וְזִכְרוֹן אֲבוֹתֵינוּ, וְזִכְרוֹן מָשִׁיחַ בֶּן דָּוִד עַבְדֶּךָ, וְזִכְרוֹן יְרוּשָׁלַיִם עִיר קָדְשֶׁךָ, וְזִכְרוֹן כָּל עַמְּךָ בֵּית יִשְׂרָאֵל לְפָנֶיךָ, לִפְלֵיטָה לְטוֹבָה לְחֵן וּלְחֶסֶד וּלְרַחֲמִים, לְחַיִּים וּלְשָׁלוֹם בְּיוֹם חַג הַמַּצּוֹת הַזֶּה זָכְרֵנוּ יי אֱלֹהֵינוּ בּוֹ לְטוֹבָה וּפָקְדֵנוּ בוֹ לִבְרָכָה וְהוֹשִׁיעֵנוּ בוֹ לְחַיִּים. וּבִדְבַר יְשׁוּעָה וְרַחֲמִים חוּס וְחָנֵּנוּ וְרַחֵם עָלֵינוּ וְהוֹשִׁיעֵנוּ, כִּי אֵלֶיךָ עֵינֵינוּ, כִּי אֵל מֶלֶךְ חַנּוּן וְרַחוּם אָתָּה. וּבְנֵה יְרוּשָׁלַיִם עִיר הַקֹּדֶשׁ בִּמְהֵרָה בְיָמֵינוּ. בָּרוּךְ אַתָּה יי בּוֹנֵה בְרַחֲמָיו יְרוּשָׁלַיִם. אָמֵן.

בָּרוּךְ אַתָּה יי אֱלֹהֵינוּ מֶלֶךְ הָעוֹלָם, הָאֵל אָבִינוּ מַלְכֵּנוּ אַדִּירֵנוּ בּוֹרְאֵנוּ גֹּאֲלֵנוּ יוֹצְרֵנוּ קְדוֹשֵׁנוּ קְדוֹשׁ יַעֲקֹב רוֹעֵנוּ רוֹעֵה יִשְׂרָאֵל הַמֶּלֶךְ הַטּוֹב וְהַמֵּטִיב לַכֹּל שֶׁבְּכָל יוֹם וָיוֹם הוּא הֵטִיב, הוּא מֵטִיב, הוּא יֵיטִיב לָנוּ. הוּא גְמָלָנוּ הוּא גוֹמְלֵנוּ הוּא יִגְמְלֵנוּ לָעַד, לְחֵן וּלְחֶסֶד וּלְרַחֲמִים וּלְרֶוַח הַצָּלָה וְהַצְלָחָה, בְּרָכָה וִישׁוּעָה נֶחָמָה פַּרְנָסָה וְכַלְכָּלָה וְרַחֲמִים וְחַיִּים וְשָׁלוֹם וְכָל טוֹב, וּמִכָּל טוּב לְעוֹלָם אַל יְחַסְּרֵנוּ.

הָרַחֲמָן הוּא יִמְלוֹךְ עָלֵינוּ לְעוֹלָם וָעֶד: הָרַחֲמָן הוּא יִתְבָּרַךְ בַּשָּׁמַיִם וּבָאָרֶץ: הָרַחֲמָן הוּא יִשְׁתַּבַּח לְדוֹר דּוֹרִים, וְיִתְפָּאַר בָּנוּ לָעַד וּלְנֵצַח נְצָחִים, וְיִתְהַדַּר בָּנוּ לָעַד וּלְעוֹלְמֵי עוֹלָמִים: הָרַחֲמָן הוּא יְפַרְנְסֵנוּ בְּכָבוֹד: הָרַחֲמָן הוּא יִשְׁבּוֹר עֻלֵּנוּ מֵעַל צַוָּארֵנוּ: וְהוּא יוֹלִיכֵנוּ קוֹמְמִיּוּת לְאַרְצֵנוּ: הָרַחֲמָן הוּא יִשְׁלַח לָנוּ בְּרָכָה מְרֻבָּה בַּבַּיִת הַזֶּה וְעַל שֻׁלְחָן זֶה שֶׁאָכַלְנוּ עָלָיו: הָרַחֲמָן הוּא יִשְׁלַח לָנוּ אֶת אֵלִיָּהוּ הַנָּבִיא זָכוּר לַטּוֹב וִיבַשֶּׂר לָנוּ בְּשׂוֹרוֹת טוֹבוֹת יְשׁוּעוֹת וְנֶחָמוֹת: הָרַחֲמָן הוּא יְבָרֵךְ אֶת אָבִי מוֹרִי, בַּעַל הַבַּיִת הַזֶּה, וְאֶת אִמִּי מוֹרָתִי, בַּעֲלַת הַבַּיִת הַזֶּה, אוֹתָם וְאֶת בֵּיתָם וְאֶת זַרְעָם וְאֶת כָּל אֲשֶׁר לָהֶם, אוֹתָנוּ וְאֶת כָּל אֲשֶׁר לָנוּ, כְּמוֹ שֶׁנִּתְבָּרְכוּ אֲבוֹתֵינוּ אַבְרָהָם, יִצְחָק וְיַעֲקֹב, בַּכֹּל מִכֹּל כֹּל: כֵּן יְבָרֵךְ אוֹתָנוּ, כֻּלָּנוּ יַחַד בִּבְרָכָה שְׁלֵמָה, וְנֹאמַר אָמֵן:

בַּמָּרוֹם יְלַמְּדוּ עֲלֵיהֶם וְעָלֵינוּ זְכוּת, שֶׁתְּהֵא לְמִשְׁמֶרֶת שָׁלוֹם, וְנִשָּׂא בְרָכָה מֵאֵת יי וּצְדָקָה מֵאֱלֹהֵי יִשְׁעֵנוּ. וְנִמְצָא חֵן וְשֵׂכֶל טוֹב בְּעֵינֵי אֱלֹהִים וְאָדָם.
בְּשַׁבָּת מוֹסִיפִים: הָרַחֲמָן הוּא יַנְחִילֵנוּ יוֹם שֶׁכֻּלּוֹ שַׁבָּת וּמְנוּחָה לְחַיֵּי הָעוֹלָמִים.
הָרַחֲמָן הוּא יַנְחִילֵנוּ יוֹם שֶׁכֻּלּוֹ טוֹב. הָרַחֲמָן הוּא יְזַכֵּנוּ לִימוֹת הַמָּשִׁיחַ וּלְחַיֵּי הָעוֹלָם הַבָּא. מִגְדּוֹל יְשׁוּעוֹת מַלְכּוֹ וְעֹשֶׂה חֶסֶד לִמְשִׁיחוֹ לְדָוִד וּלְזַרְעוֹ עַד עוֹלָם. עֹשֶׂה שָׁלוֹם בִּמְרוֹמָיו, הוּא יַעֲשֶׂה שָׁלוֹם עָלֵינוּ וְעַל כָּל יִשְׂרָאֵל וְאִמְרוּ, אָמֵן.

יְראוּ אֶת יי קְדשָׁיו, כִּי אֵין מַחְסוֹר לִירֵאָיו. כְּפִירִים רָשׁוּ וְרָעֵבוּ, וְדֹרְשֵׁי יי לֹא יַחְסְרוּ כָל טוֹב.
הוֹדוּ לַיי כִּי טוֹב כִּי לְעוֹלָם חַסְדּוֹ. פּוֹתֵחַ אֶת יָדֶךָ, וּמַשְׂבִּיעַ לְכָל חַי רָצוֹן. בָּרוּךְ הַגֶּבֶר אֲשֶׁר יִבְטַח בַּיי, וְהָיָה יי מִבְטַחוֹ.
נַעַר הָיִיתִי גַם זָקַנְתִּי, וְלֹא רָאִיתִי צַדִּיק נֶעֱזָב, וְזַרְעוֹ מְבַקֶּשׁ לָחֶם. יי עֹז לְעַמּוֹ יִתֵּן.
יי יְבָרֵךְ אֶת עַמּוֹ בַשָּׁלוֹם.

בָּרוּךְ אַתָּה יי אֱלֹהֵינוּ מֶלֶךְ הָעוֹלָם בּוֹרֵא פְּרִי הַגָּפֶן.

Baruch ata Adonai Eloheinu melech ha'olam, borei pri hagafen

Blessed are You, **Lord our God, King of the Universe, who creates the fruit of the vine.**

We drink while leaning to the left.

We pour a cup of wine for Elijah the Prophet and open the front door, inviting Elijah to come and announce that the Messiah has arrived!

Hallel Giving Praise

A fourth cup of wine is poured, and the rest of the Hallel is said.

God has remembered us; may He bless us. May He bless the house of Israel; May He bless the house of Aaron; May He bless those who fear God, small and great alike. May God increase your numbers, yours and your children's also. May you be blessed by God, Maker of heaven and earth. The heavens belong to God, but He gave the earth to man. The dead cannot praise God, but we will bless God now and forever. Halleluyah!

How can I repay God for all His kindness to me? I will lift the cup that celebrates my rescue, and will call out the Name of God. I will keep my promises to God in the presence of all His people. God finds the death of His righteous people to be terrible. O God, I am Your servant - Your servant the son of Your maidservant; You have opened the ties that bound me. I will sacrifice a thanksgiving offering to You and will call out the Name of God. I will keep my promises to God in the presence of all His people, in the Temple yards, in the middle of Jerusalem. Halleluyah!

הַלְלוּ אֶת יי כָּל גּוֹיִם, שַׁבְּחוּהוּ כָּל הָאֻמִּים.
כִּי גָבַר עָלֵינוּ חַסְדּוֹ, וֶאֱמֶת יי לְעוֹלָם.
הַלְלוּיָהּ.

Hallelu et Adonai kol goyim, shabechuhu kol ha'umim, ki gavar aleinu chasdo, ve'emet Adonai le'olam. Halleluyah!

Praise God. all you nations; honor Him, all you peoples, for His kindness to us has been great, and God's truth is forever. Halleluyah!

Hodu la'Adonai ki tov, ki le'olam chasdo.	הוֹדוּ לַיי כִּי טוֹב - כִּי לְעוֹלָם חַסְדּוֹ.
Yomar na Yisrael: ki le'olam chasdo.	יֹאמַר נָא יִשְׂרָאֵל - כִּי לְעוֹלָם חַסְדּוֹ.
Yomeru na beit Aharon: ki le'olam chasdo.	יֹאמְרוּ נָא בֵית אַהֲרֹן - כִּי לְעוֹלָם חַסְדּוֹ.
Yomeru na yir'ei Adonai: ki le'olam chasdo.	יֹאמְרוּ נָא יִרְאֵי יי - כִּי לְעוֹלָם חַסְדּוֹ.

Thank God, for He is good; His kindness lasts forever.
Let Israel say: "His kindness lasts forever."
Let the house of Aaron say: "His kindness lasts forever."
Let those who fear God say: "His kindness lasts forever."

הַלְלוּיָהּ.

In my troubles I called out to God,

and God answered me and brought me relief. When God is with me, I have no fear; what can any man do to me? With God as my helper, I will see the downfall of those who hate me. It is better to trust in God than to trust in man; it is better to trust in God than to trust in great people. All nations surround me - but by the Name of God I will defeat them. They surround me over and over again - by the Name of God I will defeat them. They surround me like bees, stinging like fire - by the name of God I will defeat them. They pushed me to make me fall, but God helped me. God is my strength and my song, and He is my rescuer.

The sound of joy and rescue can be heard in the tents of the righteous: "God's right hand does mighty deeds! God's right hand is lifted up! God's right hand does mighty deeds!"
I will not die, because I will live and tell about God's deeds. God may have made me suffer, but He did not let me die. Open the gates of righteousness for me; I will enter them and thank God. This is the gateway to God, the righteous will enter through it. Thank You, for You have answered me and have been my rescuer. The stone that the builders refused has become the cornerstone. This is from God; it is wonderful in our eyes. This is the day that God has made - let us be joyful and happy on it.

אָנָּא יי, הוֹשִׁיעָה נָּא. אָנָּא יי, הוֹשִׁיעָה נָּא.
אָנָּא יי, הַצְלִיחָה נָא. אָנָּא יי, הַצְלִיחָה נָא.

Ana Adonai hoshi'a na! Ana Adonai Hoshi'a na!
Ana Adonai Hatzlicha na! Ana Adonai Hatzlicha na!

Please God, help us! Please God, give us success!
Please God, help us! Please God, give us success!

Blessed is the one who comes in God's Name; we bless you from the House of God. God is mighty, and He has given us light; therefore, tie the festival offerings and lead them to the altar. You are my God, and I will thank You; You are my Lord, and I will praise You. Thank God for He is good; His kindness lasts forever.

Thank God for He is good; His kindness lasts forever

Give thanks to the Power above all powers;	His kindness lasts forever;
Give thanks to the Master of all masters;	His kindness lasts forever;
To Him Who alone does great wonders;	His kindness lasts forever;
To Him Who made the heavens with wisdom;	His kindness lasts forever;
To Him Who set the earth on the waters;	His kindness lasts forever;
To Him Who made the great lights;	His kindness lasts forever;
The sun to rule by day;	His kindness lasts forever;
And the moon and the stars to rule by night;	His kindness lasts forever;

We drink the fourth cup while leaning to the left.

Baruch ata Adonai Eloheinu melech ha'olam, borei pri hagafen.	בָּרוּךְ אַתָּה יי אֱלֹהֵינוּ מֶלֶךְ הָעוֹלָם בּוֹרֵא פְּרִי הַגָּפֶן.

Blessed are You, **Lord our God, King of the Universe, Who creates the fruit of the vine.**

Blessed are You, **Lord our God, King of the Universe, for the vine and the fruit of the vine, and for all the food grown in the field, and for the wonderful, good, and spacious land which You gave to our forefathers, to eat from its fruit and to be satisfied from its goodness. God, have pity on Israel Your people, on Jerusalem Your city, and on Your altar and Your Temple.**

Rebuild Jerusalem, the holy city, quickly in our days. Bring us to Jerusalem and make us happy by rebuilding it; let us eat the fruit of Israel and be satisfied from its goodness; and let us bless You for its holiness and purity. (On Sabbath add: favour us and strengthen us on this Sabbath day) and make us happy on this Festival of Matzot; for You, God, are good and do good to all, and we thank You for the land and for the fruit of the vine. Blessed are You, God for the land and the fruit of the vine.

Chasal sidur Pesach kehilchato	חֲסַל סִדּוּר פֶּסַח כְּהִלְכָתוֹ.

We have completed the Pesach seder properly. Just as we have been privileged to celebrate it this year, may we be privileged to celebrate it next year.
God in heaven, please lead Your people back to Zion in song.

Leshana haba'a biYerushalayim habenuya!

לְשָׁנָה הַבָּאָה בִּירוּשָׁלַיִם הַבְּנוּיָה!

Next year in the rebuilt Jerusalem!

On the second night of Pesach we begin counting the Omer, the seven weeks between Pesach and Shavu'ot.

Baruch ata Adonai Eloheinu melech ha'olam, asher kideshanu bemitzvotav vetzivanu al sefirat ha'omer.
Hayom yom echad la'omer.

בָּרוּךְ אַתָּה יי אֱלֹהֵינוּ מֶלֶךְ הָעוֹלָם, אֲשֶׁר
קִדְּשָׁנוּ בְּמִצְווֹתָיו וְצִוָּנוּ עַל סְפִירַת הָעֹמֶר.
הַיּוֹם יוֹם אֶחָד בָּעֹמֶר.

Blessed are You, **Lord our God, King of the Universe, Who has made us holy with His commandments and commanded us to count the Omer.**
Today is the first day of the Omer.

To Him praise belongs, to Him praise is fitting

A mighty King, chosen, as is proper - His troops sing to Him: To You and to You, To You just to You, To You even to You, To You belongs the Kingship. To Him praise belongs, to Him praise is fitting.

An outstanding King, beautiful, as is proper - His followers praise Him: To You and to You …

A deserving King, strong, as is proper - His angels praise Him: To You and to You…

A Unique King, powerful, as is proper - His scholars praise Him: To You and to You,…

The greatest King, awesome, as is proper - those around Him praise Him: To You and to You…

A Humble King, He redeems, as is proper - His righteous praise Him: To You and to You…

A Holy King, merciful, as is proper - His angels praise Him: To You and to You…

A Powerful King, supportive, as is proper - His purest praise Him: To You and to You…

כִּי לוֹ נָאֶה, כִּי לוֹ יָאֶה.

אַדִּיר בִּמְלוּכָה, בָּחוּר כַּהֲלָכָה, גְּדוּדָיו יֹאמְרוּ לוֹ:

לְךָ וּלְךָ, לְךָ כִּי לְךָ, לְךָ אַף לְךָ, לְךָ יי הַמַּמְלָכָה,

כִּי לוֹ נָאֶה, כִּי לוֹ יָאֶה.

דָּגוּל בִּמְלוּכָה, הָדוּר כַּהֲלָכָה, וָתִיקָיו יֹאמְרוּ לוֹ: לְךָ וּלְךָ...

זַכַּאי בִּמְלוּכָה, חָסִין כַּהֲלָכָה טַפְסְרָיו יֹאמְרוּ לוֹ: לְךָ וּלְךָ, לְךָ...

יָחִיד בִּמְלוּכָה, כַּבִּיר כַּהֲלָכָה לִמּוּדָיו יֹאמְרוּ לוֹ: לְךָ וּלְךָ...

מוֹשֵׁל בִּמְלוּכָה, נוֹרָא כַּהֲלָכָה סְבִיבָיו יֹאמְרוּ לוֹ: לְךָ וּלְךָ ...

עָנָיו בִּמְלוּכָה, פּוֹדֶה כַּהֲלָכָה, צַדִּיקָיו יֹאמְרוּ לוֹ: לְךָ וּלְךָ...

קָדוֹשׁ בִּמְלוּכָה, רַחוּם כַּהֲלָכָה שִׁנְאַנָּיו יֹאמְרוּ לוֹ: לְךָ וּלְךָ...

תַּקִּיף בִּמְלוּכָה, תּוֹמֵךְ כַּהֲלָכָה תְּמִימָיו יֹאמְרוּ לוֹ: לְךָ וּלְךָ...

Adir bimlucha, bachur kahalacha, gedudav yomru lo: Lecha ulecha; lecha ki lecha; lecha af lecha; lecha Adonai hamamlacha. Ki lo na'eh. ki lo ya'eh.

Dagul bimlucha, hadur kahalacha, vatikav yomru lo: Lecha…

Zakai bimlucha, chasin kahalacha, tafserav yomru lo: Lecha…

Yachid bimlucha, kabir kahalacha, limudav yomru lo: Lecha…

Melech bimlucha, nora kahalacha, sevivav yomru lo: Lecha…

Anav bimlucha, podeh kahalacha, tzadikav yomru lo: Lecha…

Kadosh bimlucha, rachum kahalacha, sinanav yomru lo: Lecha…

Takif bimlucha, tomech kahalacha, temimav yomru lo: Lecha…

He is mighty

May He build His Temple soon. Quickly, quickly, in our lifetime, soon. O God build, God build, build Your Temple soon.

He is chosen, He is great, He is outstanding; May He build…

He is beautiful, He is faithful, He is deserving; May He build…

He is pious, He is pure, He is unique; May He build…

He is powerful, He is wise, He is king; May He build…

He is awesome, He is raised, He is strong; May He build…

He is a redeemer, He is righteous, He is holy; May He build…

He is merciful, He is almighty, He is forceful; May He build…

Adir Hu Yivneh beito bekarov. Bimheira, bimheira Beyameinu bekarov.
El benei, El benei , benei beitcha bekarov.

Bachur Hu, Gadol H, Dagul Hu Yivneh…

Hadur Hu, Vatik Hu, Zakai Hu Yivneh…

Chasid Hu, Tahor Hu, Yachid Hu Yivneh…

Kabir Hu, Lamud Hu, Melech Hu Yivneh…

Nora Hu, Sagiv Hu, Izuz Hu Yivneh…

Podeh Hu, Tzadik Hu, Kadosh Hu Yivneh…

Rachum Hu, Shadai Hu, Takif Hu Yivneh…

אדיר הוא

אַדִּיר הוּא יִבְנֶה בֵּיתוֹ בְּקָרוֹב

בִּמְהֵרָה, בִּמְהֵרָה, בְּיָמֵינוּ בְּקָרוֹב. אֵל בְּנֵה, אֵל בְּנֵה, בְּנֵה בֵּיתְךָ בְּקָרוֹב.

בָּחוּר הוּא, גָּדוֹל הוּא, דָּגוּל הוּא יִבְנֶה בֵּיתוֹ בְּקָרוֹב. בִּמְהֵרָה, בִּמְהֵרָה...

הָדוּר הוּא, וָתִיק הוּא, זַכַּאי הוּא יִבְנֶה בֵּיתוֹ בְּקָרוֹב. בִּמְהֵרָה, בִּמְהֵרָה...

חָסִיד הוּא, טָהוֹר הוּא, יָחִיד הוּא יִבְנֶה בֵּיתוֹ בְּקָרוֹב. בִּמְהֵרָה, בִּמְהֵרָה...

כַּבִּיר הוּא, לָמוּד הוּא, מֶלֶךְ הוּא יִבְנֶה בֵּיתוֹ בְּקָרוֹב. בִּמְהֵרָה, בִּמְהֵרָה...

נוֹרָא הוּא, סַגִּיב הוּא, עִזּוּז הוּא יִבְנֶה בֵּיתוֹ בְּקָרוֹב. בִּמְהֵרָה, בִּמְהֵרָה...

פּוֹדֶה הוּא, צַדִּיק הוּא, קָדוֹשׁ הוּא יִבְנֶה בֵּיתוֹ בְּקָרוֹב. בִּמְהֵרָה, בִּמְהֵרָה...

רַחוּם הוּא, שַׁדַּי הוּא, תַּקִּיף הוּא יִבְנֶה בֵּיתוֹ בְּקָרוֹב. בִּמְהֵרָה, בִּמְהֵרָה...

Who knows one?

Who knows one? I know one! One is our God in heaven and earth
Who knows two? I know two! Two are the tablets of the law
Who knows three? I know three! Three are the fathers
Who knows four? I know four! Four are the mothers
Who knows five? I know five! Five are the books of the Torah
Who knows six? I know six! Six are the parts of the Mishnah
Who knows seven? I know seven! Seven are the days of the week
Who knows eight? I know eight! Eight are the days to circumcision
Who knows nine? I know nine! Nine are the months before a baby is born
Who knows ten? I know ten! Ten are the commandments
Who knows eleven? I know eleven! Eleven are the stars in Joseph's dream
Who knows twelve? I know twelve! Twelve are the tribes
Who knows thirteen? I know thirteen! Thirteen are the qualities of God

---

Echad mi yodei'a? Echad ani yodei'a. Echad Eloheinu Shebashamayim uva'aretz:
Shnayim mi yodei'a? Shnayim ani yodei'a. Shenei luchot habrit
Shelosha mi yodei'a? Shelosha ani yodei'a. Shelosha avot
Arba mi yodei'a? Arba ani yodei'a. Arba Imahot
Chamisha mi yodei'a? Chamisha ani yodei'a. Chamisha Chumshei Torah
Shisha mi yodei'a? Shisha ani yodei'a. Shisha sidrei mishna
Shiv'a mi yodei'a? Shiv'a ani yodei'a. Shiv'a yemei shabta
Shemona mi yodei'a? Shemona ani yodei'a. Shemona yemei mila
Tish'a mi yodei'a? Tish'a ani yodei'a. Tish'a yarchei leida
Asara mi yodei'a? Asara ani yodei'a. Asara dibraya
Achad asar mi yodei'a? Achad asar ani yodei'a. Achad asar kochvaya
Sheneim asar mi yodei'a? Sheneim asar ani yodei'a. Sheneim asar shivtaya
Shelosha asar mi yodei'a? Shelosha asar ani yodei'a. Shelosha asar midaya

אֶחָד מִי יוֹדֵעַ?

אֶחָד מִי יוֹדֵעַ? אֶחָד אֲנִי יוֹדֵעַ: אֶחָד אֱלֹהֵינוּ שֶׁבַּשָּׁמַיִם וּבָאָרֶץ.

שְׁנַיִם מִי יוֹדֵעַ? שְׁנַיִם אֲנִי יוֹדֵעַ: שְׁנֵי לֻחוֹת הַבְּרִית

שְׁלֹשָׁה מִי יוֹדֵעַ? שְׁלֹשָׁה אֲנִי יוֹדֵעַ: שְׁלֹשָׁה אָבוֹת

אַרְבַּע מִי יוֹדֵעַ? אַרְבַּע אֲנִי יוֹדֵעַ: אַרְבַּע אִמָּהוֹת

חֲמִשָּׁה מִי יוֹדֵעַ? חֲמִשָּׁה אֲנִי יוֹדֵעַ: חֲמִשָּׁה חוּמְשֵׁי תוֹרָה

שִׁשָּׁה מִי יוֹדֵעַ? שִׁשָּׁה אֲנִי יוֹדֵעַ: שִׁשָּׁה סִדְרֵי מִשְׁנָה

שִׁבְעָה מִי יוֹדֵעַ? שִׁבְעָה אֲנִי יוֹדֵעַ: שִׁבְעָה יְמֵי שַׁבַּתָּא

שְׁמוֹנָה מִי יוֹדֵעַ? שְׁמוֹנָה אֲנִי יוֹדֵעַ:
שְׁמוֹנָה יְמֵי מִילָה

תִּשְׁעָה מִי יוֹדֵעַ? תִּשְׁעָה אֲנִי יוֹדֵעַ:
תִּשְׁעָה יַרְחֵי לֵדָה

עֲשָׂרָה מִי יוֹדֵעַ? עֲשָׂרָה אֲנִי יוֹדֵעַ:
עֲשָׂרָה דִבְּרַיָּא

אַחַד עָשָׂר מִי יוֹדֵעַ? אַחַד עָשָׂר אֲנִי
יוֹדֵעַ: אַחַד עָשָׂר כּוֹכְבַיָּא

שְׁנֵים עָשָׂר מִי יודע? שנים עָשָׂר אֲנִי
יוֹדֵעַ: שְׁנֵים עָשָׂר שִׁבְטַיָּא

שְׁלֹשָׁה עָשָׂר מִי יוֹדֵעַ? שְׁלֹשָׁה עָשָׂר
אֲנִי יוֹדֵעַ: שְׁלֹשָׁה עָשָׂר מִדַּיָּא.

One little goat, one little goat

that father bought for two coins; One little goat, one little goat
Then came a cat and ate the little goat that father…
Then came a dog and bit the cat that ate…
Then came a stick and hit the dog that bit…
Then came a fire and burned the stick that hit…
Then came water and put out the fire that burned the stick…
Then came an ox and drank the water that put out…
Then came a slaughterer and slaughtered the ox that drank…
Then came the angel of death and killed the slaughterer…
Then came the Holy One, blessed be He, and destroyed the angel of death that killed…

Chad gadya, chad gadya:

Dezabin abba bitrei zuzei.
Chad gadya, chad gadya.
Ve'ata shunra, ve'achla legadya, …
Ve'ata kalba, venashach leshunra…
Ve'ata chutra, vehika lekalba…
Ve'ata nura, vesaraf lechutra…
Ve'ata maya, vechava lenura…
Ve'ata tora, veshata lemaya...
Ve'ata hashochet, veshachat letora,...
Ve'ata mal'ach hamavet, veshachat leshochet…
Ve'ata Hakadosh Baruch Hu, veshachat lemal'ach hamavet...

חַד גַּדְיָא, חַד גַּדְיָא

דְּזַבִּין אַבָּא בִּתְרֵי זוּזֵי,
חַד גַּדְיָא, חַד גַּדְיָא.
וְאָתָא שׁוּנְרָא וְאָכְלָה לְגַדְיָא...
וְאָתָא כַלְבָּא וְנָשַׁךְ לְשׁוּנְרָא...
וְאָתָא חוּטְרָא והִכָּה לְכַלְבָּא...
וְאָתָא נוּרָא וְשָׂרַף לְחוּטְרָא...
וְאָתָא מַיָא וְכָבָה לְנוּרָא...
וְאָתָא תוֹרָא וְשָׁתָה לְמַיָא...
וְאָתָא הַשּׁוֹחֵט וְשָׁחַט לְתוֹרָא...
וְאָתָא מַלְאָךְ הַמָּוֶת וְשָׁחַט לְשׁוֹחֵט...
וְאָתָא הַקָּדוֹשׁ בָּרוּךְ הוּא
וְשָׁחַט לְמַלְאַךְ הַמָּוֶת...

How does it work?

**We used different three dimensional methods in this haggadah.
In order to get the illusion of a real three dimensional object, we need to space apart the eyes so each eye has different view. The seperation is made possible, using the dual colors of the glasses. The brain then puts the two pictures together to create one three dimensional picture.**

Creator, 3D Producer: Michael Medina
Sculpture and Painting: Emi Sfard
Photography: Eli Neeman
Graphic Design: www.pirsum4u.com
English language Editor: Elli Fischer
Hebrew language editor: Zehavit Ehre
Produced & Published by KIPPOD3D

Thanks:
www.miniatures.com
Ehud Gros - Minisrael
www.minisrael.com
Pinchas & Clara Sover
Medina family
Hirshhorn family
Dana Gordon

See you next year